MW01598821

A disgruntled Disn
Supervixen are a fe
myth, architectural ...., ... draws
inspiration from Catholic saints, garage bands, the Seven African
Powers, performance art and the history of lipstick. Whether its
characters are fasting in the desert, casting spells in suburban kitchens,
or losing an eye in the gender wars, *Tear Down* takes a wry and
visionary look at impermanence, the meaning of home, and finding
solace in a fallen world.

To Heather,
Thanks for cmj
to the 2006 launch!

Peace!
[signature]

Also by Ali Riley

Wayward

Tear Down
Ali Riley

Frontenac House
Calgary, Alberta

Book and cover design: Epix Design
Cover art: Meghan Hildebrand
Author photo: Alan Chong

Library and Archives Canada Cataloguing in Publication

Riley, Ali
    Tear down / Ali Riley.

Poems.
ISBN 1-897181-04-3

    I. Title.

PS8585.I438T42 2006   C811'.6   C2005-907651-8

We acknowledge the support of the Canada Council for the Arts which last year invested $20.3 million in writing and publishing throughout Canada. We also acknowledge the support of The Alberta Foundation for the Arts.

 Canada Council Conseil des Arts
for the Arts du Canada

Printed and bound in Canada
Published by Frontenac House Ltd.
1138 Frontenac Avenue S.W. Calgary, Alberta, T2T 1B6, Canada
Tel: 403-245-2491 Fax: 403-245-2380
editor@frontenachouse.com   www.frontenachouse.com

1 2 3 4 5 6 7 8 9 11 10 09 08 07 06

For Noam Ash

Acknowledgements

Thanks to my family. Deep gratitude to my mother, Fern Hunter, and love and respect to the memory of my Nana, Dorothy Merrill Prynallt and my father, Douglas Gerald Riley.

For advice, feedback and kind words I would like to thank Anne Waldman, Quincy Troupe, Jon Paul Fiorentino, Billeh Nickerson, LuAnne Armstrong, David Bateman, Tom Wayman, Stuart Ross, Ian Samuels, sheri-d wilson and Michael Turner. Luisah Teish's *Jambalaya* and *Lies* by John Newlove continue to nurture and inspire.

I would like to thank the Canada Council for the Arts for their assistance.

Thanks also to: Anne Green, Melanie Little, Nicole McGill, Jeff and Alison Pew, Terry Taylor, Sean McGarrigle, Nancy Jo Cullen, Travis Reynolds, Jack Dylan, The Electric Tractor, Pharmacie Esperanza, Hector Navarro, Mamba Racine, Shanti Yoga Studio, the Kootenay Shambhala Centre, Jade, Peter Churchill, and Gerry Hill for the "Wandering Eye".

Love to my cross-country brothers and sisters. You fill my heart and inbox: Clay McCann for the title "Sermon of the Fire Ants", Heather Fox, Coen, Ainsleah "the Scarf" Hastings, Aja Rose Pea, Carolyn Mark, the In Flux kids, Pam Klaffke, Natasha Shannon, Crucial Bunny, Chandra Mayor for "poppy as big as a fist", Randy Zimmer, Stew and Giselle, Pony and Tony, Meghan Hildebrand, Tankia Makasoff, Josh Wapp, Vladimir Sobolewski, Tarran and Nayana, Laurie Siblock, Doc Edge, the ghosts of all the dwelling places, Anosha, and always and always Sanny.

Many thanks to Layne Coleman.

And to the ancestors. *Selah*.

Some of these poems previously appeared in: *Event; This Magazine; Matrix* and *Moosehead Review*.

Contents

My Sister, Guard Your Veil
7 easy pieces

There are a few women who are so full of the force of life, they don't ever need a push. They're not delicate, and they're feared and rebuked for it...behind their back.
- Lisa Crystal Carver, *Rollerderby*

*I look down at sweet teresa's convent
all those nurses, all those nuns
to me you know
they look pretty damn free down there*
- Patti Smith, *Piss Factory*

The female function is to groove—be herself, explore, discover, invent, solve problems, crack jokes, make music—all with love. In other words, create a magic world.
- Valerie Solanis, *Scum Manifesto*

For Each Man-Eater a Lady-Killer
for Tura Satana, Phoenix, 1973

Allah picked up the golden sand
and cast it to the wind
saying:
they shall fly without wings.
  - The Koran

1
in every western tradition
(save consumerism)
I am
considered a whore

at a sixth grade Valentine's dance the big Okie kid
in the corner said
stay away from her
she's a Man-Eater

we were in the backward class
played third world
to the governing body of gifted faces
I didn't want
to develop

my blood buzzed locust-like
my buxotic body was dry land
bereft of exploration
run over me like Georgia
I said to Sherman-boy
colonize me

2
a tough rose
blooms anyway
steeped in Jericho sand

I painted bat wings on my eyes
I crushed He-man spine
I kicked at the sky
my ship-shape held and redirected the light
sparkled the air around me

3
a film student asked Russ Meyer: *What are your influences?*
he said: *World War Two*

a fox-hole
hankerin'
for benevolent flesh

4
he visits often, itching to maul
his hands can't wait
his heart keeps making excuses
for his inclinations—
I love her
he says as he takes the stairs two at a time

   only look

see how I scry the floor
see how I keep my head down,
so tears drip straight and don't spoil
my pretty
pasted-on eyes

my twin pugs sit at the foot of the bed

   regarding me like sultans

my salve is sleep
I clutch it always
after he takes
his leave I take it all in
the compensatory joy of sand world

the sandman leads me out of sticky-wet Mudville
to a parched holy place, the dream desert

   yes, there are weapons under the dunes

5
I have always loved the dark-haired strangers, the lady-killers
desert men, people of the Book
these men of G-d
so quick to anger
devotion
prophecy

the sultanate pugs speak of me fondly—
she's hot as an iron, one says
a fevered girl is better than no girl at all, the other replies
besides, she could easily be made cold if that is what you prefer

they laugh

6
the flash makes daylight brighter than ever
the planes drop their cargo
turning the desert to glass

Insha'Allah

my tears flow and are whipped away
by cleansing grains

7
my skin is polished
no fingerprints remain

I am glass

take my heart—
it's too big
for my triple D chest

Empty Box
for Samantha Stevens

1
tears+blossoms=tincture

it must be the sex
the Witch-World says
why else love a mortal
a dull mortal at that

they don't understand
the pull
of projection

everything I hold
dear
I can pour into you

2
Tabitha tries to make her blanket
stand on end
but it will not
it consistently slides to the floor
she cries
she summons all her sorcery to defy physics
she consults her Esso™
Book of Everyday Witchcraft

Magick won't work like that, I say
that's just what blankets do, they lie

3
new moon tonight—
it's very dark out there
you say, wiping your boots
as the dog runs first through the door
you've been gone three hours
it's obvious he hasn't been walked

I dream a full moon
just to remind myself
you'll come back
the worm will turn again

I'm real watery, see

    Pisces rising

I know how to surf
the ebb and flow
the push and pull—
the disastrous cold
after a heat wave

4
we mirror each other's isolation:
I wait at home
    I contain multitudes
you are out on the town
    vacant

some women can't help but ask the unanswerable:

What's wrong?
What are you thinking?
Do you love me?
What do you mean?
What about last week at Galaxy Fest when you said
I was Counselor Troi and Princess Leia rolled into one?

5
the truth of envy:
I want what's yours
the ability to move

that good gooey thing
the blind eye
to the wake of squalour
the body that can only face forward
you're a laundry flat

the trick of never looking back
bland, practical
your gaze fixed on the next meal
set precisely at six
joyless, yes
but devoid of howling

6
the priestess arrives
I point to
my invalid womb
as if it's the *Sacre Coeur*
and I am the Virgin Mary
    please, sister
    save the baby

her hands hover
perform
a makeshift mudra
the arms of me empty
    walls
    cave
    towers
    crumble

a spell in the air
can't pull its own weight
witches have no TV clout
only the powers of
root, herb and stone

7
I figured out penis envy—
it means that you are getting suntan lotion smeared on you
while I haemorrhage for three weeks
and ponder
the etymology of the term *scot-free*

I've lost my powers
I've lost my steel
I need iron
in my heart

my blood freezes
into cubes of ice
to add to the grape juice

anti-communion
awash with spite and control issues

8
I confess—

I was in league
with beasts and reptiles
locked eyes
soft kisses
the serpent turned warm for a time
and made his own kind of sense
a blanket statement
a graveyard gesture
no lawyer's looks could have prevented me
from falling

I'm looking to make a deal:

I walk out of here

"Yea I Know, Nothing Stays in My Body"
for Tracey Emin

the veil is gone
snakeskin passed over my eyes
you burned holes
in my cellophane

hereafter
you would excise me
sew me up with sinew

this prospect has me
dancing on pins
    an angel, every one of them

the point ends in blood
on the crinkly pad of the gurney
    lies

the bones that moved
through me
this day
in July
    why do they let you flow so freely?

what came
quickened and quit
I will name:

    Julio

and be filled
with the tentative zeal
of a fever-broken child
gorging on jelly

Snow White Spills
Anaheim, 1999

Welcome to Over-Stimu-Land. I'm sick of it all—the herky-jerk Lincoln that makes the kids cry, the vomitous primary colors of my outfit, the free samples of icky sticky gelatin brought to you by Vitamin Upjohn—*eww*. Bile-melt. A chemical blob…plus there is a split-shift evening Troll that is seriously impeding my ability to think straight.

Lately when I come to work numbers keep popping into my head, how many jobs, apartments, men, how many lipstick containers are landfill because of this stupid gig. I can't work here much longer. Luckily I'm top of the Princess pile—the Dwarfs are humanoid, if theoretically eunuch. Cinderella, all she has are house mice. Beauty is the worst—like a '50s housewife on Benzedrine. Objects coming alive, the Beast asleep in the next room and she's all, *Candlesticks are singing to me! Teapots are giving me advice!* I zip my dress and hit my trademark stride, my lips unwaveringly crimson, my hair getting darker every year, against all odds.

There are rumours of a Secret Room here, probably Masonic. *Why?* This is the place where every child begs to go. What if some of them are "lost" and taken to a Secret Room? Fitted with tracking devices? Chosen, marked, *tagged*—to walk through life troubled, sought out, like the freak magnets they will eventually be. I bet there *is* a Secret Room in the Kingdom of the Mouse. Invisible lines of connection that implicate the highest office in the land. Not to mention Kris Kristofferson, and someone also told me Willie Nelson, but I don't like to think of him as doing all the sex stuff, probably he was just drinking in the kitchen.

Oh yeah, they've got it all. The Pop Princess, the Boy with the Iron Nose. Man, they've probably got a real unicorn down there. It all boils down to—*listen*—the guys that run this machine are *men*, you know? You don't think they'd have scientists and G-men working around the clock to create the perfect sex slave?

I'm just surprised *I* haven't got a call.

Always the Demonic Sorceress, Never the Bride
for Courtney Love

1
wall+drama (fist+plaster)=hole

slippery heart
slooshes groundward
tripped over
accidentally kicked somewhere
under the stove
down a vent

welcome to my dwelling place
for that is what I do—
    don't dwell upon it
    they say

each room has a purpose
the kitchen always and always for wailing

2
within these walls I take a stab at you
I want you to let me in
my shortcut knife only disappoints
as your bellyful slides to the floor
you elude me once again
  gutless

I can't leave
I'd walk but I'm squatting
and without this shack
I am nothing
only skin and hail

my soiled lace shucked
on the floor, I glue
patches of hair on myself
I want to be a Magdalene
on the Good Ship Wallow

3
In this ramshack of rasp
    this sugar shanty

I cough out dust
try to get you
out
of my lungs

    the overflow of my sahara heart

4
soft heart

O spare me
the kitchen
histrionics
this is no Movie of the Week
my despair's not quite
camera ready
so dance me a storm

I'll dress like a widow
   the sorrow of the ladies
walls are talking
   newborns and the wizened
whispering wives tales
   the oven, always the oven
the tear-stained carpet, the residue
everything becomes landfill
families

   a withered aunt

5
restraining order
on a/trophy wife

> *babies*
> *didn't keep those poets safe*

prepare for saints
the daemon says
hex yourself

no matter how ghetto-fabulous
your Hollywood home
there will always be coyotes in the canyon

Ladies of the Canyon
for the Magdalene

1
heller in pink net
tights I was Christ-like
a fisher of men

once caught, they are released
each encounter necessitates its own trip
back to the badlands

I must again repair
to the desert
grow strong
on locusts and honey
land-locked
dreaded
gun-cocked

I return
with a sword
an ax
with nothing
but my hands and a hole

in God's earth

I wait
for the precision of a wave
that never comes
a fugue that does
        does the radio talk to you?
I irradiate joy

(explosion)

2
the Sacred Harlot comes
to the healing circle

Christ
not another cad

at the last supper
He ignored her in front of His friends

I want my own disciples
she thinks

3
meta-whore sees
her body as metaphor

    a temple
    a convent
    a place

to hang
Your head

walls are just walls
a room isn't real
until you pour Love
into it

4
I could not resist teasing You
I needed Your eyes on me

I needed all men's eyes
like dirt under my nails
like meat between my teeth
a high-heeled stumble-through

> *the room opened up*
> *the sky was there*

Interior Castles
for Saint Teresa of Avila

1

life's blood spilled=passage to heaven

beware of archers
I was told

sloppy hunters don't care
where their shafts fly
where Eros
ends and you begin

beware of arrows
I was told

once shot you're stuck
    walking carrion
babbling in kitchens
    you're left

years after
he will brush against you
to push his point further
to make sure the spikes still hold
you will ask your God
the question
of prophets and losers:
why me?

Born March 28, 1515. Her mother's family crest has a burning tower, from the day the Christians took Castile back from the Moors. Her father's side is descended from *conversos*—forcibly converted Jews. At five her favourite game is Hermit. At seven she runs away with her brother to get beheaded for Christ. Their plan is to walk to the land of the Moors, tell the Infidel they're Christians and have their heads chopped off. They leave with a handful of sultanas in a handkerchief.

2

my country the most powerful in this world
    de Soto searches for the City of Gold
    mowing down millions

I'm never going back to its many masters
    cyanide in children's eyes
    for the sake of something shiny

or the toothless cowards
    fortunes made in machetes

not to the boats that leave every day
looking for the dark
    spices   *slaves*   *cocoa*
and the light
    sugar   *cotton*   *diamonds*

I have put myself out of the mercantile loop
there is nothing we Brides can't do
for ourselves
in our spare
cloth
alone with sprintly
thought

Avila is a city of walls within walls, a gated community. Women are veiled. Some wear the *tapado de medio ojo*—a veil that only covers one eye—enabling flirtation when in public. After her mother dies, Teresa, 13, has a brief glam period—she piles her black hair high, wears an orange dress, and spends a lot of time with those she later calls *frivolous cousins*. Her father places her in a convent two years later. She throws herself completely into convent life, and even though she is plagued with health problems, she receives raptures and visions. She writes about them in her book, *Life*.

3
O to be sainted
sisters keep you in line
the way a team of brothers never can

O to be Teresa
seized up
eyes lifted
she receives
golden arrows
of fond-faced putti

her mouth
    agapE
her back arc'd
    a covenant

The Inquisition seized her *Life*, then ordered her to write another book. Illuminists were under scrutiny, females especially. The *beatas* were disdained as "foolish women" by authorities— hysterical, dangerous and possibly in league with the Devil. In *The Interior Castle* (*Book of the Dwelling Places*) she keeps wistfully referring to the book she lost. Her main concern, though, is the grace of God and how one may go about attaining it. Throughout the book runs the fear of loss of grace, of the Devil appearing as Divine Light.

4
one look at the face of God=15 years mediocrity

His advances now cold
I perform my duties
for 15 years
rewriting a book already written

just give me
a missive
a mission

　a word

Does she feel abandoned by God? She confesses a doubt that He came to her in the first place. She's so humble, almost to the point that you get mad at her. You wonder if she's just covering herself for the Inquisitors. Perhaps that's a modern way to see it. Tortured in love, there can be no doubt she gets Him in the end.

The Boyfriend Sutras
108 Performances

To tell the truth and to shoot well with arrows—that is Persian virtue.
  - Zarathustra

…exploring the physical and mental limits of her being, she has withstood pain, exhaustion and danger in the quest for transformation…
  - Press Release, Marina Abramović's *7 Easy Pieces*,
    Guggenheim Museum

Psychotic women—they abound.
  - Art Bergmann

Girl, You'll Be a Woman Soon

a song of beauty
as they wrap the
fish
net
around the little girl's neck

playtime in half-built houses
we are climbing to the ceiling
write our own script
in pencil crayon
ballooning on the raw boards
till dry wall
plaster
    divorce
    dust
makes a seamless show
to hang a portrait on

Love is the Reason I Loathe Geometry

two lines have no choice
but to run parallel
never touch

        or

intersect
and
move away
into infinity

Let's make up our own rules!
we say

there is always gravity
to trip us
the law of rubble
and ditch

A Honey Mistake

1
don't talk to me about the Promised Land
not now, not ever

milk and honey are not free
though they lack the outward
       yes boss
drudgery of sugar
       white death
bees in thrall   cows in stall

2
men cut cane
       your uncles
then came
the first victorious speech of the Revolution
when the released dove
flew back onto Fidel's shoulder
charmed the Cuban crowd

Ochun! they whispered

3
You, master
of malaprop
roll over and say
work is for the bees
you are the laziest man in town
and still you leap
over me at the crack of noon
to e-maul other women

I left your bed
passed you on the porch
still lounging, cup of takeout
the mouthful I took much too sweet
a honey mistake you said

I had my first at a café around the corner
Cuban organic, reminded me of you
no spoons, so I poured and hoped for the best
I gave it too much
when I mentioned it later that we must have
made the same mistake at different times
you said, *that means I'm under your skin, babe*

4
don't talk to me about Revolution
the pine-scented Che that hangs
from your rear-view mirror
can't camouflage the smell of cold feet
of nothing worth dying for
your untrammeled, unparticular appetite

5
please don't talk to me about Rock n' Roll
babies in Ray-Bans™
and dogs with Frisbees™ killed it
please never—no never—play *Stormy Monday*
the Blues™ are a franchise
owned by the Terminator
cold curly fries make me nostalgic
for woody bootleg poison

depression-era lost hope
is so much more amazing
than your velour robe

6
BJM Anton says—
Get ready for the revolution, baby!
There's two kinds of people in this world,
those with a loaded gun
and those who dig. Dig?
my thoughts immediately run
to Elmer Fudd and Bugs Bunny

I can't talk to you, period
I feel like Joseph Beuys
smothered in gold leaf and honey
explaining pictures
to his dead hare

7
I, gringa girl
fix a jar of honey for Ochun
to entreat her
to enchant you
the cards say: *the desirous leper must charm the fool*

I add spices from India, from the Islands
5 cinnamon sticks, 5 cardamom pods, 5 cloves

there is a price on the tiny heads
of all these things
I am so selfish

    I want your eyes on me

Red Thread

An invisible red thread connects those who are destined to meet, regardless of time, place or circumstance. The thread may stretch or tangle, but never break.

   - Chinese Proverb

1

We left things dangling, the loose ends a cat o'nine tails. No satin ribbons or silken threads hold me. I am tethered by a Jethro belt. Nylon, yellow, utilitarian. The kind that must be burnt—hard plastic meltdown—to keep from unravelling.

Your name is Russian for *Prince*. Mine is Arabic for *Exalted One*. It should have been gravy, we should have been covered.

Your bland exterior baffles me. *An empty box,* I think. A red square, a line of soldiers, a fresh red-coat for every downed man. You admit you build walls, but you're just the contractor. I am interested in the architect. If I can trace the plan, read the blueprints, I can solve you.

I shapeshift, become raven, and I'm back near the Steppes—some disputed and unclear boundary where your ancestor Prince Something waits for battle with his men. The soldiers are bored, talking target practice. The Prince brags he can shoot the eye out of a raven. This is what he is famous for. It's on your family crest. *Slepy Wron.* One-eyed raven.

I am annihilated—blinded for future lives, when all I see are your good points and miss the danger.

2

Our past and parallel lives poke into the present. They run with us, a marathon of sigh and shiver. You're in *On the Waterfront* longshoreman drag. I'm all Ice Princess in purloined fur and red eyeliner. Our heads together, kissing in the corner. Clay told me, *You looked like deposed Russian royalty at the party last night.* He pronounces us *He and She.*

ROLL FILM:

St. Petersburg: We are pledged to each other at eight and five. When we kneel in front of the priest—veil over both our heads—you are twelve. I'm fifteen, bored as a baby-sitter—*just get taller or something*—and it's rough games in the hallway until your growth spurt hits and we make love five times a day. You accept my surrender—*O wife O body O my plunder.* Dirty-faced escapees, we arrive in Paris. Under assumed names we peel potatoes and wash dishes.

Oneida County: We are Perfectionists. Noyes' experiment in Christian living. Eighteenth century group marriage. I am in the kitchen bouncing babies with the other wives. The utopian Woodstock moment before the Altamont of stabbing jealousy.

Kentucky: called by Shawnee *the dark and bloody ground.* You made a beautiful general. When I saw you ride bushy-haired towards me, I couldn't resist rising above my servile station, acting the plantation queen and pulling my calico close. Even your horse stared. You kiss exactly the same way, wherever we find ourselves. This night it's my moon-time. We are bloody as a battlefield. You hold your hand to your face and paint it for combat. I mark you, red ends up everywhere. *I want to go with you,* I say. *I'll give you men who want to rule the world.* A wink and a toss, your image

fades. Bright light. The filmstrip melts up the scenery. Headache-white.

3

Wars and rumours of war, an infection we pass between us, back and forth, an incurable disease. Poison gas entered my Grandfather's lungs—*mustard crazy*—snapped him forever. The family choked for years.

Men took your father—on their collars the rune *Sowelu* doubled, twin suns—and killed joy with a sick *schadenfreude* belly-laugh. Shiny car, architecture of doom. Sudden movements, heavy steps, a door flies open—

If I ran back in time, burnt the battle plans, busted out like Bruce Lee, stopped the blows and bullets—*then* could we love?

You are Russia. A red night. A rival country. Though greatly changed and seemingly harmless, there are many iron angels still pointing at my heart.

4
should I blame the Prince?
an arrow's sole purpose
is to fly
connect

a life means nothing
in a constant state of quiver

Memory

You want an answer to everything!
says yesterday's e-mail

perhaps I once was your Inquisitor
perhaps you once were St. Teresa

I dissect every sentence
to find the heresy of contradiction
I read back what you said yesterday
every time you change your mind
I check my ledger

should be made of human skin
or sacrificial lamb
something important-looking
to tote
off to the rack
to the bleeding room

now I see
I am the supine one
there are scribes waiting to take down
everything I say
that is why I feel insane
when I speak of your inconsistencies

because you are reasonable
you hold the pen

You/Mine/Me

you are glitter
to my jaundiced eye

I was a new penny
I lost my copper
I lost my worth
now I am nomad
eyeless in organza

pirate-patch
a dusty bandage
industrial flesh-tone
covered by a child's
Jolly Roger

you in a copperplated tower
baldheaded, name of Rapunzel
no way to get to you
nothing to hold on to

other men still want me
as I rollicky-trudge
up city sidewalk
up grades

the fear of the wandering eye
is not that it wanders
but that it sets
on you

Strong Silent Type

you write your name in me
a staggered-staccato
Morse code
    secret plot

you speak low
or not at all
    silent salvo
    dumb, fluttery praise
you trace letters on my
perfect
place

not the consonant-heavy
Balto-Slavic of your father
too poor to buy a vowel

you doodle
you sew
a quilt of
Ah—Ee—Oh

in the sly
Latin undulate
of your mother

fat filigree tongue
of *coups d'etat* and ex-communicants
    the ever-present Inquisition

Hausfrau

Women decorate with an eye to how the world should be. *Mother of Pearl*, *Arms of Mary*—what is worse than the dresser-top detritus of a man? His clutter is driving me mad. While he works out of town I redecorate. *I want magic.* I fuss around altars. I arrange things. A pebble, a smudge stick, heads of the Virgin. I place bits of bone, second-hand fur and Nana-bling, put glitter everywhere. This is embarrassing, but I like to decorate and cook. It's something I really know how to do. Growing up, in my family, a wife was not considered a decent thing for a woman to want to be.

*

Men decorate with representations of themselves. See, that's what guys don't understand. You wonder why your girl-roomie keeps moving your plastic Frankenstein toy back to your bedroom—even though it's the only object that's yours in the realm of pink-fluff and faux surfaces. The plastic toy is so *male*, so clearly *you*—monster hands held helpless in front of your face.

Well-meaning kitten-strangler. Unwitting child-murderer.

*

You call. The date is made. I wait on the back porch. I practise meditation though I'm not fit to breathe. My throat seizes with larcenous wow and flutter. My heart pounds like a shoplifter's. I maintain outward silence, try to fight the gibbering brain-innards of monkey-mind.

*

The lady next door waters her Astroturf™ while I wait for you. She sprays the sidewalks, goes to the bay window and polishes her Hümmel figurines— Dutch children kissing. They remind her of the Old Country. The distance between This *und* That. A place where everyone behaves behind lace curtains. A flat-earth world outside these treacherous ranges.

*

A woman's memory is spiked silver claws piercing a mattress, Freddy-style. Show-dog sex is *my* Old Country. We war horses are ponies that never forget a trick.

*

I continue to wait, dry-mouthed, for the black reeds and uncharted marshes of your body. The sun is scary, so I wind-bathe in the shadow of a cedar. I am hungry to delineate your spacious gaze. I flip through *The Mapping of Canada*.

A rumble of thunder perks my ears: it could be crunchy gravel. A reason to run, poodle-like, to the picture window.

You arrive. You smile. I walk away and you catch my sleeve like stucco. Your twinkle disappears with the promise of a riding. Your eyes matte with porno-glaze. *Shell-shock.*

*

We lock and roll. We are our own stunt doubles. We step into our lost sluttiness like a Comeback Special, Liza-style—arms outstretched—*thank you*—in the spotlight, promising the crowd *I'll never leave showbiz again...*

An affair is a playground, not a house. Show-dog sex keeps our hearts safe. We pull all our old specialties out of mothballs. Later I hide my ripped knickers at the bottom of the trash can.

We are triple digit, triple threat. Man-Eater and Lady-Killer. Cannibal and felon, both former addicts to the Playing Field. We left the Wide World of Sport long ago but today we are *Soop-ah-Stars!* Of slag. Of shag.

...because you've always led such a sheltered life

Dinner that night—our boundaries ill-defined—we sit opposite in hard chairs. The fence between us so long and tall we don't know which one of us is in jail.

I try to explain again that in this love I am the boys and you are the men in helmets.

the Heart is a lonely long-distance runner

You were such a lucky boy, but you wanted to be luckier. Range-fed and tight-boxed. You climbed trees to knock out the baby crows. Your stick-play: legendary. Your back-woods talk: believable. You took in stray glances and registered them for later. You chalked names on your blackboard heart. Easily erased, easily banged out behind the portables.

I was shy girl. Stayed inside. Grub. Bookworm. I could be the new pointless craze—I could be pet rock. Gag gift. A couple of googly eyes stuck in a gray lump of over-handled dough. A raisin mouth. Bloomless baby.

I'd like to believe I'm sitting on a gold mine. Body, check. Head, check. Heart, somewhat intact. The heart—long-shot winner of all the races. *Woo!* Limping into first, the other contestants dead on the field behind. Shot by arrows—whose? Someone romantic enough to want the heart to win. Otherwise, raw need could take it. Guts. Any nameless organs that could be fried up for extra iron and whatnot. Let's not even discuss *brains*. Or top-of-the-pole, much revered reason. Drive.

Cut everything down to size—hell, lobotomize—and you still got that reptilian stick-to-itiveness to contend with. Lizard man. *Lizard man.* There just aren't enough Leonard Cohens to go around.

One Woman Show

Thousands of lipsticks. 108 boyfriends. 40 apartments. 1 psych ward question: *Do you receive messages from the television or the radio?*

thousands of lipsticks

I came from a lipstick family. The women brought me into their Touch and Glow world. Many shiny surfaces in which to judge yourself. My mother's *Holiday Magic.* My Nana wore the same shade for years until they discontinued it. *Apricot Velvet,* then *Adobe Coral.* Her widow's austerity products—Noxema, Listerine, King James Bible and Zest—didn't keep her from her Revlon. Even in the old folks home, she re-applied every time she went to the dining hall. The day before she died, she held a smushed tube in her right hand, *Softshell Pink* smeared everywhere. *This lipstick isn't working,* she said.

I don't believe the gesture of glamour is merely an expression of sexual fear. I came from a lipstick family. Spaghetti westerns made me thirsty for green stockings. I fed the dance hall girl inside, played stagecoach with neighbor boys—a pretend strike by savage arrow, a fast roll down the hill, Timmy Royer (as the Doc) taking the pulse of my lily-white when I came to a halt. *She's dead,* he'd say, looking up at the others. A man who loves you. A compelling destruction. An abiding wish.

108 Boyfriends

Show and Tell, grade three. I brought a crab claw from a King Crab. *My friend the King Crab,* I began. From the back of the class came a southern drawl, *Why did you eat him if he's your friend?*

Outside the school, grade six. He is waiting for me with his Export A cigarettes and his denim jacket. He pushes me up against the brick wall, holds a cigarette to my face and makes me yell, *I am a pregnant platypus. I am a prostitute!* When I tell my friend about it, she says, *Oh, that means he likes you.*

We lived in a squat on Hastings, by pigeon park. Woodwards had yet to fall. Einsturzende Neubaten (German: *collapsing new buildings*) perform at Expo. Billed as *A band of young people from Berlin,* they play their power-tool anti-oom-pah-pah to an aghast crowd. Every time I get spam—*break down walls with your big cock*—I think of him. There were barriers between us no big dick could smash. I see the penis as Post Industrial now.

I said nothing as I passed him, just shoved the lemon from my drink into his mouth. He took it well, ape-man Godfather style, minutes later coming over to my table and presenting me with a dried rind. In a high-rise pagoda, the jilted Columbian next door sings someone's name in a language made for sorrow. Red and black negligee in the elevator, peeking out of a paper bag.

He took me on a bruise wheel vacation. We glazed the walls lilac. He spray painted my name, and the word *bitch.* I washed off the marks with Javex™ and Varsol™. I want to be clean.

We met cute, during a police raid. He was flicking his Zippo. He lit me. *Nice trick, did you learn it in jail?* I Ava-snarled into his Sinatra-smirk. We each had our *noir* up. We got our bikes and rode three blocks. Later he said he fell in love with me when the condom made a noise hitting the floor and I said, *I wonder how Don Martin would've spelled* that?

His name a famous one, a knife on the page. An obsessive twang. *You won't hear me speak it.* Famous stabber, heads on spikes. Dictator. Legendary devil.

40 apartments

I wish men were like apartments. When you move in, you see all the things that jar your eye. A mismatched piece of carpet, an exposed pipe. You're going to paint this and cover that. After two weeks or so you don't see the flaws anymore, the vile tub, the stain on the curtain. I am drawing diagrams, making plans. I think about measurements. I think about wood, elaborate guises. Building block, safety net, tightrope, drywall. The spook of houses, of electricity. We are wired for trouble. I can feel it in my teeth.

endless drama

I don't have boyfriends. Boyfriends, no. I have associates, accomplices.
We plot my destruction together. The talk shows and colourful books in
airports say I should be about tactics. I am a no-good general of my heart.

Two generals meet in a cabin. Their troops wait anxiously outside.
They've been out of rations and walking barefoot in the snow for weeks.
Ragtag slither machine, old men and boys.

My breakups are not messy, no. They are performance art. Some sky-
dive, or wrestle gators, I am a flying Wallenda of spite. No net. Clothing
set on fire, a camera smashed, illicit photos glued to the wall. In lipstick,
on the bathroom mirror, GONE FISHIN.

one psych ward

Every time you take a pill, it's a symbol of someone caring about you.
L. Park and L. Cori (1965) Archives of General Psychiatry

End-of-your-life waste management. So many questions: *can you add 23
and 44?*—roll up your sleeve please—*Can you tell me the meaning of the
phrase make hay while the sun shines? Do you receive messages from the
television or the radio?*

the message, CBC Radio Late Night:

he is unable to talk
or gesture
and yet, the Vienna Symphony Orchestra
responds beautifully to him

Wishing

you are the pit
into which
I cast my

self

and hope
it will turn out
well

The Dwelling Places
6 Structures

*I am amazed at how this great wealth—spirit
has made its home in this poverty—body.*
  - Gospel of Thomas

*Never thought I'd miss the National Hotel
Never thought I'd see the day*
  - Lost and Profound

*The awake lion prowls for God in places
he once feared.*
  - St. John of the Cross

1st Dwelling Place
National Hotel

Nature of Dwelling: Corporeal. Inglewood. Brick and mortar. 4 storeys. 9,988 square feet. Still standing. Converted to condos.

Architectural Details: Hardwood floors, CPR pension, green metal chest of drawers. A blood stain in the bathroom shaped like Huckleberry Hound doing something to a teddy bear. Smoker's hack, false teeth in the urinal. Peg-leg pants, *London Calling*, chicken bone necklace. Buckskin skirt, Clairol Blue-Black, Tempo Truck Stop. Boom town busted, *Too Drunk to Fuck*. Dances with winos.

African Power: Elleggua
AKA: Papa Legba
               Trickster
               God of the Crossroads

Attributes: red and black
               possum, rooster
               corn, candy, rum
               crooked stick

Sainted Equivalent: Archangel Michael
Lipstick Colour: Tibet Red, Ochre de Tyre
Chakra: Muladhara, base of the spine, survival, root centre

Floorboard Undervoice: There are few dwelling places in His castle in which the devils do not battle. - St. Teresa

Calgarian

It begins with a field holler. Robert Johnson makes a deal with Ellegua at the crossroads. Music mirrors the noise at hand. Chicken scratch barnyard dance—Maybelle Carter. Train hop-and-chug *now I got nuthin'* rhythm of the Delta. Post-war post-traumatic widow sob-sounds of Hank. B-52 bombers, hot-rods and Hendrix. Computer keys and Depeche Mode. Eighties dance: hands to the side, palms against the sky—think an overly florid Bowie *Heroes* pose—shielding oneself from the nuclear rain.

It begins with a turntable, a glass of warp-speed
flavour-ridden numbskull paint thinner
listening to Metallic KO alone in a rec-room
quarter taped on the tone arm
the first Ramones album—*escape*
punches a hole in the suburban sky

It begins with trading your birthright
for torn t-shirts, three chords and a bash on the head
from Billy-Jo Gunrack, buzz saw guitar in a tiny bar
sign on the 8th Avenue entrance:
no belt buckles no knives no colours

not the wheat, not even chaff
we are citizens of Garageland
the semolina 1%

My glitter obsession got me through grade 8. The smarmy anti-glamour of Lou Reed's *Berlin* and photos of the New York Dolls—with their blue-black sticky-up hair—prepared me for the ultimate—Patti Smith's *Horses*. I couldn't share my discoveries. My friends liked Led Zep, Aerosmith, Rush. I wanted a Lester Bangs friend, a baby crow-beau of my own. A couple of years of hitchhiking yielded one record store clerk in Kamloops who knew who Rimbaud and Patti Smith were. So, like everyone else I would soon meet, it was me and my records in the basement.

Limbo Pad

band house named after catholic nowheresville
it was all about the space between things
a place of no definition where anything goes
no boundaries, the Maw, and the name of the place is
I like it like that

we didn't know the move was born on a slave ship
the dip-below-the-chain of a stolen people, a will to endure
Yoruba, Dahomey, Ibo
the most genius shadow cultures to ever live
kept their Gods alive in a new brutal setting
they made the *loa* into saints and kept the real names secret
whisper/code/rhythm
we owe our music, hence our lives to you
Alafia

in a house named limbo
we dance secret dances
sing secret songs

Virgin Prunes boy prostrate, blocking the bathroom door
in high heels and '50s cocktail dress
Guitarsplat shaves his head with a Lady Schick
Cy Alexandria, swathed in black velvet,
runs the redneck gauntlet to score more beer

we huddle under the radar
the tainted wind blowing North
from underground tests

The Nuclear Clock was at one minute before midnight. Parties were apocalyptic. We knew
we were the last generation. Sinatra said *Don't let the Blues make you bad*. Jeffrey Lee
Pierce—hallowed son of a Mexican manicurist—said *Take the Blues and turn it into suicide*.
We found family in a world of shoulder pads, stockbrokers, and Duran Duran.

The National Hotel

as we unload band gear
-40 Farenheit blizzard
3000 miles from CBGB's
I recall my first train hop
at 14, trip-terror jump—
off at the Nat'

kind craggy faced flop-house then, built for the railway
the dream, the spike
men lived here who could put away a whole steak
in seconds
now dust buddies

tonight the rooms are filled
undernourished guitar players in black
some thrown in the drunk tank
Cree dude cackles
what's a Hutterite doing in jail?

all these ghosts will haunt the coming condos
as sure as the bones of the ancestors
still taunt the covered wagons

Cadaverous face, the biggest hair. I once made a child cry just by walking on the LRT. That hyper-pumped, seat-on-the-Gold-Exchange time *needed* a spectre in its midst. Ditto all the downtown piss-tank rednecks who hassled us every day, a bone-deep rebel-yell, fake laugh six inches from your face. Screaming *what the hell is it?* Threatening sudden 2 x 4 violence. DIY safe zones. *You best be coming home to me before they drop the bombs/wedding bells in the shelter of your arms.*

2nd Dwelling Place
House of Chango

Nature of Dwelling: Non-corporeal. Dreamscape

Prevailing Winds: Primitive Ballet, acid rain. *You can't help who comes to you.* There is no place for hesitation on the battlefield. Slashed wedding presents. Glossolalia. Guardian devil.

African Power: Chango
AKA: Shango
           Xango
           John the Conqueror
           macho king
           lover of women
           protector of orphans
           Lord of Thunder

Attributes: red and white
           horses, rams
           double-headed ax
           castles, lightning, fire
           apples and yams

Sainted Equivalent: Barbara
Lipstick Colour: Coco Red, Hibiscus
Chakra: Swadhisthana, sexual centre

Floorboard Undervoice: Let us strive to do what lies in our power and guard ourselves against the poisonous little reptiles. - St. Teresa

The Chango Sutra

the drawing

I made a stick drawing with sword and crown and called it The King. At the time I knew nothing of the African Powers. The *orisha*, the *loa*. I idly embellished him, as if in a trance. His long shoes—a grotesque parody of rockabilly cat. A dick-to-the-ground stalactite of splendour.

the dream

I married him in a dream, the African king. A Protector God, speaking from a tower, He steered me clear of tainted alleyways. I was His wife and accorded all rights and privileges, though I do recall having some trouble with the headdress. This warrior came to me in my days of rage, of running into roads, naked under London Fog.

He came in snips, in half forgotten daydreams, reveries and lyrics. I had yet to learn all His attributes, but already had a life-long attachment to some of them—castles, red and white gingham, and horses. In waking life I wear black, but one day am compelled to purchase yards of red and white gingham. That night, at an opening, a man in white face and Aleister Crowley t-shirt hands me a glass of whiskey and a palmful of mushrooms.

Poison! I scream, hours later, my arms around a tree that's dying in its sidewalk cage. *Poison*! I clutch my bag, see gingham everywhere. That night I dream once again of the African King. He tells me his name— *Chango*. In the morning I figure I've channelled him from the WWF. There's a wrestler called Poppa Chango.

the confirmation
It took a Cuban to set me straight
the boyfriend of Marie-man
He is no wrestler, m'ija, He is Chango.
He will give you Aché. That means power.

the protection
Hector, priest of Chango, calls. He tells my machine, *I wish you Aché.*
He warns me to be careful. *However kind, never forget—Chango is also a*
fucker. Oye, Chango, you walking contradiction, you. Patron of orphans,
fighter of fires, winner of court cases—and macho pimp.

In any language if a girl is, as Kazantzakis says of the Magdalene, *covered*
with the sweat of all nations, she is in need of a protector. She moves
beyond protection, she relinquishes it. Irma La Douce *poules* have their
protector/pimps, to them they are one and the same. *This is the game*
that moves as you play.

the contradiction
Wow. These African Powers really keep you on your toes. *Kabiosile.* The
problem with a Protector God that is also a Fucker is that you never
know where you stand. To what extent He will protect and to what He
will destroy. When it seems He failed you, you think of ways it could
have been worse.

the manifestation

This man is *carnevale*. A stone heart in a stubble field. He's cotton candy, sweet and dangerous. His father says, *he is rough, he gets excited, but he is soft inside.* Red blood cells. White blood cells. Be my Valentine. Ah, assassination.

He gives me a dagger. Perhaps he does not know how to be fond. *Watch out for this one*, Ochun says. *It's written on his face: possession.* Yes. I recognize the raised brow, the dimple. The wild eyes. But he is stuck in fear and not rolling with the *loa* of his *abuela*. He gives me the no gift fake-out. He says everything could change. He says take another step. He says go away. I call him *Querido*, I say *por favor. You're still as lovely as before*, he says.

I say: *Words can't hold you.*

3rd Dwelling Place
Symptom Hall

Nature of Dwelling: Corporeal. Claremont Street, Toronto. Wood and beam. 2 Storeys. 1,672 square feet. Torn down for condos.

Architectural Details: Cat piss basement, booze can, *Mellow Gold.* Communication through Drag. Prozac™ capsule glued on forehead as bindi. *Everything I Needed to Know I Learned in Junior High.* Shooting up phosphorus. 50¢ Fashion show, *Slanted and Enchanted*, late-night slice. Opium tea, bicycle wobble. Capitalism makes deserts.

African Power: Ogun
AKA: Ogu
              fierce old man of the woods
              warrior

Attributes: green and black
              wooden staff
              goat, dog
              machete, iron
              handful of nails
              roots, nuts, berries, meat
              railroads

Sainted Equivalent: Anthony, George
Lipstick Colour: Film Noir, Russian Red
Chakra: Manipura–*jewel in the city*, Solar Plexus, courage, power centre

Floorboard Undervoice: Little security: it is necessary to test ourselves. Sometimes He withdraws. - St. Teresa

Affinity Group Found

We began in water. Our first core-group experience was skinny dip—climbing the public pool fence at Christie Pits. Two girls, straight. Two boys, gay. A sudden crowd of Latino adolescents hissing *pusssssy*, fingers through the chain fence. We girls grabbed towels, they posed as our boyfriends, got us out of there quick-like. *How Suddenly Last Summer,* Albrecht said. *If I hadn't talked to them in the language of their mothers, it would have been really bad,* Marie-man said.

In between: blood, earth and copper. The women eat sunflower seeds, have two-hour analytical phone calls, and love the unsuitable.

The men go to Boyztown.

We converge at Sympton Hall, where the heavy black stage curtains become my confessional.

We ended in water, before all the splits and in-fighting. It was Marie-man's belated birthday, and we blindfolded him and took him to the country, stopping on the way at a crappy bakery. *The slave wants a donut* he kept screaming. Fricka and I swam in a lagoon. A father and son suddenly appeared in a canoe. *This little one sees things,* the man said. *You will be rewarded.* The boys ate and took pictures that later startled us with their pre-Raphaeliteness.

We called ourselves the Turner Family after the Bitter Old Queen in *Boys in the Band.* (He snaps at Errant Guest— *You're* TURNING, *dahling.)* I met them after I got dumped for a vapid VJ.... I had made a pact with myself—if it doesn't get any better in two months, you can die any way you like.

Symptomatic

Das Rheingold/ An Industrial Opera /Opening Night 1994

I am crawling through broken glass, half naked, with a pig's heart in my mouth. It does not once cross my mind, doesn't cross anyone's mind, to wonder what we are doing here.

An Equity person comes by with some contracts, takes one look at the set and says it's the most dangerous production he's ever seen. Among the hazards:
—a six foot pit in the floor
—a sack of fluorescent light bulbs that come showering down at the beginning of every performance.

Fricka has a leather hood, says Herr Direktor

—is that baby going to be on stage?
—stage blood that covers the floor in the first act is slipping hazard, especially since two of the cast members are on stilts
—ditto the rotten apples.

You mean *The apples of youth?* says Herr D.

I will do anything to turn his head. I am the girl in the trunk, I'll be the girl in the ditch. All to the soundtrack of *Live Through This.*

Albrecht was diagnosed today. Fricka says we should keep it to ourselves. I think Herr D. needs to know so he doesn't run Albrecht around too much. We have a lot of physical stuff. Albrecht says no, he's OK.

Everyone should have the opportunity to join a cultish group headed by an Alpha Madman. If it doesn't end in suicide or mass murder, it's something you will recall fondly the rest of your life. Das Rheingold is said to be the Scottish Play of opera. In every production someone goes mad. This time everyone went mad.

Herr D's wife is the stage manager. She is tiny and exquisitely pretty. Every night it takes her hours to sweep up the broken glass and stage blood and re-paint the floors white. I feel bad for her, but it also means I can have him to myself for most of the evening.

That we played the truth game at all, let alone that day, was a surprise. The cast was demoralized and resenting Herr D more than ever. We played a game with metaphors that had to do with everyone at the table until Albrecht put the kibosh on it by saying, *And this person you're talking about, when they cut themselves, how long does it take to heal?*

The shock of the sudden. One morning your neck feels funny and next thing you have a life filled with expensive machines, unfamiliar logos. Siemens. You hold stats in your head like an adolescent baseball fan. You are symptomatic.

Herr D is seeing omens everywhere. Yesterday he stopped rehearsal because a paint chip appeared in the floor. *It's in the shape of a dark angel,* he said as he had us gather around it.

Mike Harris became premier in 1994. The WTO formed in 1995. I remember someone saying, *I had my first political thought in years today.* It was the "Tomorrow Belongs To Me" in the beer-garden moment. Every family has the glue that holds it together, but Albrecht was more than that. He made the world seem friendly.

Cabin Fever

We were all looking forward to a weekend in the country. I, at least, pictured something that resembled a BC style cabin—outhouse, dirt floors, log walls— but instead it is identical in every way to a large, suburban house. It *is* a large suburban house. It feels enough like being in the country that we discuss who would survive if this was a Slasher film. Of course it would be Fricka—she's the single one. Since Goblin dumped her on Monday, Fricka has not stopped crying all week.

Saturday afternoon the doorbell rings. It's the woman from up the street and her two kids. *Just wanted to say hi, how's it going!* Mijnoon makes awkward small talk in the kitchen and the kids race into the living room, where we are having coffee, languishing like sultans. The youngest sucks his ring finger and stares at Fricka, sobbing in the corner. The oldest looks at Marie-man through the wrong end of her toy telescope.
-*You're just getting up now?*
-*Yes.*
-*Why?*
-*Because when you are getting up, we're just going to bed. And when you're eating lunch, we're just getting up.*
She lowers the telescope. *Kind of as if you lived in China.*
From beneath his quilt on the couch Albrecht says,
Yes. We're very productive members of Chinese society.

Less than a year before Albrecht died we had lunch near his apartment, in the courtyard at the AIDS hospice on Church. There were a bunch of birds pecking crumbs, and he was feeding them. One came jumping up, all black and spiky and fucked-up looking, like it'd been in an oil slick. Albrecht said *Oh my God, and what happened to you ya little freak?* and made sure the other birds didn't drive it away. Albrecht gave us courage. I will speak his real name here because his name is what he did. *Mark Shields.*

the beginning of the almost-here end

opportunistic virus+architectural clear-cut=prime real estate

All the old-school bakeries are going out of business, now the Laundromat is closed. There's an official soon-to-be sign in the official corporate colours, blue and yellow. Underneath is a small, hand-written one: *we wanted to keep our Laundromat. we are very sorry. we are very sad.*

There are rumours of condos. Of the gambling debts of the landlord. *We've been lost in a card game,* they say. *That sounds so spaghetti western,* someone says. There are men on the street screaming into cell-phones. Albrecht hasn't crossed Bathurst in weeks. Too sick.

There is this: it will fall
hip dysplasia
we are very sorry. we are very sad.

there is also this:
buildings shake, walls tumble
dirt stays grounded

During one of the Days of Rage marches I realized I had to leave the city. I was convinced there would be some kind of riot or something else horrible. The final straw was being attacked one day by a tweaked out would-be gangsta-girl. By then, The Turner Family had long since passed. Herr D had a new cult. I visited him at Symptom. I told him I was leaving town and grabbed a beat-up wood table from the basement. I'd always thought it was so beautiful, it reminded me of Saskatchewan. I called it the Farm Table and kept it through dozens of moves and apartments. It sits today in the kitchen of my farmhouse.

4th Dwelling Place
House of Ochun

Nature of Dwelling: Non-corporeal. Dreamscape.

Prevailing Winds: Written by a girl-child in pink felt on an orange piece of paper, the top star qualities: Glances of withering scorn. Concern. Poetical attitudes. Political attitudes. Being relaxed. Passion. Vibrant, distinctive cosmetics. Composure. Balance between conceit and self criticism. L-O-V-E.

Ancestor dream-guides, stage setting, the beckoning Valley. Global warming. *Dilatasti cor meum.*

African Power: Ochun
AKA: Oshun
Maitresse Erzulie
Freda-Dahomey
the love goddess
the party starts when she arrives

Attributes: yellow, peachy pink
parrot, vulture, peacock
mirrors, fans, gold
honey, cinnamon
Cuba

Sainted Equivalent: Our Lady of Caridad del Cobre
Lipstick Colour: Rocker, Viva Glam

Chakra: Anahata, heart, love, compassion centre

Floorboard Undervoice: The important thing is not to think much, but love much. - St. Teresa

The Dream of the Ancestors

Ochun. I know She is my *loa*. Party-hopping Valkyrie, Sacred Harlot, pumpkin for a purse, sweet Queen of clear rivers. The coquette. The glam. Oh *you*. She'll bring you love, you can ask for anything, but watch out for Her sense of humour. There is often a blade under Her petticoat.

Ochun and Chango are great lovers. Together They conceive the Ibeji, the Divine twins. Some say She is His wife, others say no, Obba is His wife, Ochun is just His favorite mistress. Whatever. They have a heavy, flirty, sexy thing going, OK? She puts Him in His place, She's got His number, She knows what a womanizer He is. Hector, priest of Chango, sighs. *Yes, that is the way it is with me and Ochun.*

*

Peacocks swallow poison
and take it out on their feathers
but the vulture is really my bird
yes I'm sweet, I tint my cheeks
with the blood of my enemies

*

I prepare a feast for the ancestors. I cook and set a plate. I call on Ochun especially. She brings me a dream. I am floating. A bend in the river, scent of cedar and dripping trees.

She brings me to a house. *It is these non-corporeal dwellings that teach you who you are.* Red and black drawings on the doorway. In the basement I meet them all. Totems everywhere of this and other lives. A chill in the air. Ancestors of all stripe, and a girl in the corner in red and white, not speaking. Ochun says, *She envies you this life.*

5th Dwelling Place
wiDe loAd

Nature of Dwelling: Corporeal. The Valhallas, BC Interior. 100 square feet. Plywood shack painted forest green. *wiDe loAd* spray-painted in orange. Still standing.

Architectural Details: Wood stove, outhouse, propane, sink for grey water. Unpruned apple trees, 4 x 4 garden plot. Ponderosa pine, cedar, hemlock. Box of MAC makeup, *Legends of the Flying Heart Tribe.* White-tailed deer, brown bear, nettle, St. John's Wort.

African Power: Yemaya
AKA: Imanje
            Agwe
            Mother of the Sea
            Womb of Creation

Attributes: blue and white
            Shorebirds, conch shell
            Silver
            cornmeal, molasses, watermelon

Sainted Equivalent: Stella Mari, Star of the Sea
Lipstick Colour: Dubonnet, Redwood (a tone)
Chakra: Vishuddha—*poison-free place*, throat, communication centre

Floorboard Undervoice: Walk with care. - St. Teresa

Spring of Falling

In the country, the terrain is more uneven. *All eyes upon you.* I went out with the Dutch guy who owns the Murder House. At the mill-workers bar, flirting and playing the juke, he got mad at me when I ordered a round without having enough to pay. Beer came out my nose when I thought of the term *Dutch Treat* (no treat at all). I pulled out my sparkly change purse and dumped all my dough to prove a point.

I had on Paramount back-lot Street Urchin look: pink gingham dress, green gingham hair-bow and 6" wooden platform wedgie-clogs. I was sassing around as we left, tripped on a pebble and broke my kneecap. The universe conspired and I complied. I was in the mood for losing, for throwing things down.

The moment of shatter. My life trotted by. He: model citizen. Me: empty-pursed, holding my knee. Psychodrama parking lot. Girls holding other girls' hair as they puke. Fights and scenes. Parking lot as Temple of Stark, the place between where we are and where we're going. We lurch out and soon we're stopping on the highway. Trees: crisp, real. Night: blurry with chaos.

Stopped at the side of the road, life rushes in. Nature—something you drive through to get to another pocket of civilization—is now in your face. *Pull into a skid, get sucked into the drift.*

I spotted a plywood shack between the highway and the river, *wiDe loAd* spray-painted on the side in orange. After my broken knee heals, I move in. No running water, no electricity. Propane fridge, outhouse, candles, fetching water with a bucket, and bathing in a lagoon.

Ill Conceived

The hippie circle baby shower. The survivalist divorcee says the blessing *to celebrate the coming birth* blah blah blah and without changing her tone *this celebration which was supposed to take place at my house then it was totally taken over by Esther*—looks exchanged around the circle. More women arrive and hug. *Blessings.* We confer blessings upon each other here like Quakers. We form a circle and weave a web—a piece of green wool round everyone's wrist, connecting us. Then we snip and now all of us have a yarn bracelet to wear until the baby is born.

An elfin, red-headed toddler is wandering around. He has odd teeth—pointy and metallic-looking. He's constantly baring them. *That's Starsha,* Esther says. Starsha looks at me and gnashes. *The night he was conceived I was in Arizona and an emissary from the Big Dipper wanted to incarnate. An Entity with blue skin and five eyes.*

Wow, I say. Starsha is biting a stick in half. Esther says, *I could only breast feed him for a couple of weeks— his teeth grew in right away.*

Later, very stoned, Marie-man gets right up in my face and whisper-shouts—*I'd stay away from that Starsha.....thing.......if I was you. And by no means ever be alone with it!*

I plan to bring my citified taste into the country. I buy Sally-Ann dolls to spray paint silver and nail to wall-wall. *It's my Kootenay Proj', mon!* Mad outskirts-living woman is my model. When I hear some animal (wolverine?) under the cabin at night, I blare the floorboards with my battery pack stereo—a blast of *Nine Pound Hammer.* Take *that*, beast! I look into the dark from the propane-lit inside, only to see my own terror-eyes wide in the glass.

Sugar Shack

The cut on my finger, where I gouged myself with the spring-loaded hair claw, is like a little mouth, singin' sad.

I'm the kind of girl that likes to wear makeup home alone. I flirt with myself in the mirror: *hello, potato pancake.* I hold cellular memory of many things: southern steam cotton worn thin, pictures of saints and pop-stars glued directly to the wood paneling, calico dress, gingham, pigtails, aprons, galoshes, fathers in underwear howling in the boat in the driveway.

Our generation's role models were hillbillies, ghouls, junkyard men and sweathogs. I worry I am the Village Goth. Fetching water gets more difficult as the river gets lower. Last week the bucket cracked.

Meanwhile, two more dead, this time in corn country. Another kid showed up in a dark trenchcoat. His classmates said, *Whattya gonna do? Kill people?* And he did. Marie-man said, *Jesus, it's like one of your plays come alive—hands up, who wants to die?* Are there going to be more and more people going insane? At Kootenay Y2K meetings, I can never figure out who is truly deranged and who isn't.

The pastor said, *Growing up on a farm, I'm not much of a media person.* Nowhere Safe: A CBC Special Report.

I told Marie-man about the cut on my finger. I said, *You wouldn't think you could cut yourself on a hair accessory.* He said, *You could cut yourself on a beachball.*

There's a bear I'm sharing this space with. Every day there are new signs—scat, broken branches—but he keeps a respectful distance. A dimly remembered semi-dirty book comes to mind, Canadian probably, and I dream him as a Victorian suitor, waistcoat and watch, *Alice* style—something else on his mind besides courtship. Better fish to fry, but the next day, on the hemlock path to the lagoon, there is an offering, a trout.

6th Dwelling Place
Murder House

Nature of Dwelling: Corporeal. A bend in the Slocan River. Pillar and beam. 2-storey, built into bank. 1,300 square feet. Still standing.

Architectural Details: Former pit-house, built by Sinixt, of the Arrow Lakes Band. Documented as burial ground. Rebuilt, cantilevered and arrogant. Northwest garden snake, skunk cabbage, lupine, cougar. Train tracks, antique wheelchair, chicken coop. Raised garden beds, WWOOFers. A crop you don't talk about. *The river sees all, takes all.*

African Power: Oya
AKA: Yansa, Aido-Wedo-Brigette
        Amazon
        Mother of Mind
        Winds of Change
        La Duena de la Cemetaria

Attributes: red and purple
        sheep, locust
        copper
        horsehair switch
        eggplant, red wine
        9 pennies

Sainted Equivalent: Teresa, Our Lady of Candelaria
Lipstick Colour: But my lips disappear without lipstick
Chakra: Ajna, third eye, command place

Floorboard Undervoice: I have had a great deal of experience with learned men, and have also had experience with half-learned, fearful ones; the latter cost me dearly. Courage: the trials begin. - St. Teresa

Call Before Pedro Creek

When we came to the valley we made it
a bored road trip child game called *Murder House!*
you call when it comes into view
at Pedro Creek you get ready, it's not as easy as it sounds
the game holds something
an old stink in a security blanket
a fetish

we stop in the blizzard, so I can pee at the side of the road
the bend in the river where the Murder House sits
a being stands static in front of me
a portal to another life
the man on the side of the road
angelic child/guardian devil
I lurch while I pull up my jeans, call *Murder House!*

then—like a kid on the fringes of the playground
glimpsed in a small moment who eventually becomes your
chief
tor/mentor
the murder house grew and grew

Marie-man and I were in different cities, but through a road trip beatnik-y meet-up we passed through the Slocan Valley and fell in love with the *Twin Peaks* meets *Woodstock* vibe. Y2K was coming, people were freaking out. Marie-man, convinced of the veracity of Y2K, had a vast store of various lentils, was thinking of buying a generator. I am at the motel village Karibu Kabins, then at *wiDe loAd*. At Y2K meetings we find out the story of the Murder House. It was a grow-op partnership gone wrong. How we heard it, when one partner came to ask for the money, *Dude just shot him. He crashed through the glass patio doors and died on the back porch. Dude panicked, gave his 12-year-old stepson a bag of pot to clean up the blood, and took the body away to bury it...*

Visiting the Murder House

It was not even my dwelling, I was a vassal from down river. The minute I walk through the door I instantly recall the interior, the house from my ancestor dream.

We hang out a lot, the owner and I. Despite his Krishnamurti sense-talk, he will often make an animal of himself. Once he grabbed the phone from my hand and ripped it from the wall. He tends to slam doors. He screams.

At healing circles I didn't know how to be:
techno-dancing, bindi-wearing, forest-walking joie de vivre
or
downshifting, trash-talking, trailer-dwelling crime spree

I knew about city crazy. People's dads moaning in the kitchen. The one who quietly and methodically lit the garage ablaze. Another who lay in the driveway, disrobed and drinking, crying ancient angry tears.

But Valley lunatics were *sane*: the biblically named prospector who showed me how to skin a dog with a golfball; the sweet-faced Solstice hippie girl at the healing circle who squeezed my hand and said *we're sisters, so we process things differently* as the alpha would-be cult leader droned on and on; the trickster-boy who lived in a yurt with three goats. As Raven, he made fire without matches, and taught me wildcrafting.

...It turns out Dude buried the body on the victim's mother's land; so he goes back, digs up the body and drags it in his truck... but there's where he gets caught, and convicted of murder and offering an indignity. We met the new owner Hans at a party, he invited us over. Marie-man and I were agog. He shows us the bullet hole on the living room wall, and the place out on the porch where the body landed, blood stains and all.

Wildcrafting Downriver

I've been praying, shedding some river-tears
there'll be plenty of time to cry
when things are dried out and dying

picking St. John's Wort I store the sunlight
I've been crying some river tears
a strum/thumbed tune sung to keep the bears at bay

pinch blossoms off the bush
honeysuckle yolks, the pollen
turns my fingers red as a tongue-sucked lozenge

a bloodless spider, miniscule, white
I brush the creature out of my bowl

a sliver of sunlight a speck of a soul
will pierce a drizzly day
a taste of tincture's dark red drop
will burn a hole in the snow
will animate and conjure the tears, the blossoms
the beat of heart
the way I swelled and swooned
pinched and plucked a late summer's day

One morning, on the murder porch, we discussed my life. I couldn't shake the feeling that I'd gone horribly wrong somewhere—ancestral vision or not. Hans said, *You have to remember you're as welcome in this world as anyone. What did you do as a child?* I sighed. *Went off in the woods. Rode my bike. Made potions.* He put a coffee in front of me. *Maybe what you need to do is dress in black, sit by the river and cry for a year. Very funny,* I said. *I'm serious,* he said. The talk ended in undue... not tawdriness, but some kind of morbid quality that I can't quite put my finger on, like hearing a noise and not knowing whether it's mouse, mechanical failure or nightmare locust.

the propane fridge froze everything

You pass a plywood shack in the middle of nowhere, *wiDe loAd* spray-painted on the side in orange. *You wonder, what would it be like to live in such a place?* And now I do: no running water, no electricity. Propane fridge, outhouse, candles, fetching water with a bucket, and bathing in a lagoon.

In isolation, I crave cafés, street-life. I'm neither here nor there. I keep finding my way to the Murder House, walking abandoned train tracks in the hot sun, the tangles of snakes parting before my thudding self.

I chop my hands to blisters making beanpoles, weeding, making myself useful. My presence, as coy as I can make it, a school marm in training, black ribbon bow-tied round my lily-white. Next thing I'm sitting on a stump and he's describing his plans for an arrow-shaped tree house shooting through the trees. He grabs me. I am the serpent, distracting him from honest labour.

A maniacal stare, a crease down the middle of his forehead, a schizoid scribble, making the porno-glaze seem the most winsome of winks. I am in sullen defeat. And now I'm back at *wiDe loAd* (*Oh Lord! Stuck in wide load again!*). I hear something in the cabin, too scared to look. It's freezing, I have no burnable wood, just big useless disks of cottonwood. I would become a murderess for a bath.

A new day, and the red gingham kerchief I tie around my head is making me feel strong and capable, in a Doukabour, Loretta Lynn kind of way. Love the land, love your coal mining man. Cha;nt: *Hark, the arrow in the immense void.* Chant: *Hey sugar? Who you calling* IMMENSE?

I started crying in the kitchen, the same kind of existential soul searching big-life-crisis bawls I always dredge up over there. I was silent-sobbing and wiping my eyes on his sweatshirt. Hans suddenly went and bolted the door and hugged me for awhile before leading me to the porch (where the body fell). He had moved his mattress outside for the heat-wave. He started kissing me and told me I needed to talk to more women because *Men get horny.* After it got dark we finally fell asleep.

That was the night

I went on the drift, but I'm paying for it. Too sick to draw water, shockingly hot to the touch, but frozen, frozen inside. Icicle stabs of panic every time I move. I long for the coolness of a thermometer under my tongue, confirming my infirmity.

the night of stumble
the night that kills you is the night
you can begin again
chant: *om namah shivaya*

Shiva: *I am become death*
destroyer of worlds

The Jericho Rose:
Its flowers and leaves drop, its branches dry and curl,
its roots retract from the soil.
It becomes a ball,
allowing the winds to carry it elsewhere.

tumbleweeds fall, they have no breakable spines
even the wind can be ocean given the right set of intoxi

build me up tear me down

He woke up and dragged me out of sleep. He kept slamming me into the wall. He kept saying GET OUT but he wouldn't let me... he wouldn't let me leave. He hauled me down the front steps and threw me onto the ground. Onto the car. Again and again. Then came... the giant concrete stairs to the river. I knew I would never survive that tumble. I brought myself up, you know. And in that moment I flashed incredibly fierce. Enough to shuck him off, jump naked and drive.

Tear Down
40 Conversions

All houses dream in blueprints.
 - The Silver Jews

Used to be people would pick you up off the floor, give you a place to crash
and a peanut butter sandwich.
 - Iggy Pop

I open up my wallet, and it is filled with blood.
 - Godspeed You Black Emperor

Crows aver that just one of their kind would suffice to tear down heaven.
This is certainly true, but it doesn't prove anything—because heaven
signifies: impossibility of crows.
 - Franz Kafka, *Observations on Sin, Suffering,*
   Hope and the True Way

Curtains Laced With Diamonds, Dear, For You

old cash registers
a bell (B major)
when the drawer opens

brisk
a cleansing sound wave
    demons disperse
I dearly miss this ping
of transubstantiation
when life's blood becomes liquid asset
paper becomes goods

an intimate act
everyone knows exchange is dangerous
    moment of joy=1 pint bodily fluids
don't put that quarter in your mouth

we are unprotected
stand nuptial-close
at the kiosk
ATM
no ringing bells

Reno on the Block

the heiress looks at her feet and smokes
her garage sale is too dear
> *teapots*
> *silver*
> *sequins*
> *gold*

the locals leave ashamed and crumpled
ungrounded, the renting class
crawlspace spine curled inward
a bent spoon
> *you can't shine if you come from tarnish*
> *no antique pram for* your *baby*
> *your empty bottles*
> *your crap footwear*

her swoosh-shoes
are sewn by small hands
her gold hewn from iron
> *machete fortunes*

when worlds collide smiles freeze
icecaps melt
the sun is harsh
> *so are we*

crabgrass cowers
in the face
of Round-up™
and I, too, fear
the pesticide glance of her

Unspeakable

in the age of advertising
we must assume
everyone is lying

shark babies, all of us
schooled in swim

the video years made us brittle
rewound and rewatched
till the mention of what we feel
sounds dead
stilted
cheese
you'll always have a place in my heart
is good for an eye-roll

it's all been there, done that
we apologize in advance
for laying it out in a meat-rack kind of way
cliché double time
barrier

put a sock in it

I awake to the ghost of neighbours present

Karibu Kabins: December 6, 1998
fault line+side of a mountain= landslide
something cracked
trees slide into the river
stuck until Highway #6 is cleared
jovial knock/Come on over man/13 points of contact

He: a face lifted from a barbershop quartet, faux earnest and basso profundo, calm landscape manner, fault lines invisible until earthquake-level rage shakes it up. He's landlocked, but he's a seaside-seeming man, used to gibber and gloat. Something's fishy about his tales.

She: a mincing cow, tip-toeing on a barbed wire fence. Limbs skinny, with the sudden visual thud of hoofy platform boots. Pre-alcoholic barrel-body. I like her. As the film noir bitch says, *we're all sisters under the mink.*

The smell of bleach and they're on it, crackling brown in a glass pipe. It wonks them, sends them madhouse. They go savage and watch beer cans move as if they are claymation.

Secret patterns of bedspreads are what every child knows from their reveries. I count faces in the fake wood paneling. Bad memories a well-walked trail. Pain pathways etch-a-sketch your brain. I am reminded of the catatonic guy I saw in the opposite booth last week. He kept spilling his food and saying *sorry daddy sorry.* Something drips from him—tears or sweat, I can't say. He's stuck in a difficult moment, forever.

His childhood home equation:
roof over your head+food on the table=father's rage
table! roof! table! roof!   Here comes the floor.

7th Dwelling Place
Ephatha

Nature of Dwelling: Non-corporeal. Castle in the Air. Safe house.
Virtual-digital agrarian. Pre-Christian Obatala. Post consumer waste.
An abundance of unmarked doors.

Prevailing winds: Red-winged blackbird, snowy owl, coyote, full moon.
Lion-faced dakini. *We adorn ourselves with birds, plants and deer,*
breaking a commandment to remind ourselves of the dirt. We don't speak
of paradise, don't name ourselves or our ways.

African Power: Pre-Christian Obatala
AKA: There is none. Obatala is Obatala

Attributes: Peace
                white and silver
                doves
                coconut

Sainted Equivalent: Our Lady of Mercy
Lipstick Colour: I am wearing my salvation
Chakra: Sahasrara—*thousand petalled lotus*, crown of the head,
universal consciousness centre

Floorboard Undervoice: Jesus touched the deaf man and said, *Ephatha.*
The man said, *What? Ephatha*, Jesus said. *That is, be opened.*
- Mark: 7:34

Age of Forget/fullness

her church has burned down
Sunday school haven
1930s chocolate and moss linoleum
basement
archaic toys

   little let-down bird
attaches to beam and frame
and is inconsolable
she knows what is coming

   a cashless society—
love doesn't hold nails in wood

in a grey rapturous vault
a heart is cloistered without benefit
of clergy or confessor
it rides on a boosting machine
a vacuum pumps slowly as the bottle fills

the last living book
in the library of the Eschaton
between the pages
a poppy as big as a fist

sermon of the fire ants

entwined in antlers and friend fairies
I was happy with my guardians
I was dressed as a silver haystack
found a new rose

we go back to the dunes
as a family this time
the desert fathers say
pray for the gift of tears

the dictator puts his lips to my ear
tells me stories of the old ones
border disputes
a turncoat priest
cousins becoming
stateless

a widow's circle of rouge
intentional?
dolls of childhood or just *look at me*

we say a blessing
that outlasts
the heat of the meal

Harvest

dangerous machinery
drives me
like Deere

give thanks
nothing I live or play with
can tear me limb from limb

Photo by Alan Chong

Ali Riley's first book, *Wayward*, was shortlisted for the Gerald Lampert Memorial Award. She was born in Calgary, and was the singer/songwriter of the seminal psycho-country band Sacred Heart of Elvis. In Toronto, she acted in several theatre productions, including *The Lorca Play*, for which the company won a Dora Mavor Moore award for best performance by a female. Her produced plays include *dog dream*, *Philosophy in the Bedroom* and *Hole in my Heart the Size of My Heart*. Her poetry has appeared in *Geist*, *The nth Position Anthology*, *Matrix*, *This Magazine*, *Event* and the *Moosehead Review*, and she has performed at festivals, schools, and hootennannies across the country. She currently lives on a farm between Nanton and Vulcan, Alberta.